TAKING CONTROL

What If You Had the Power to Control Your Destiny?

Shayne Hammond

BALBOA.
PRESS

A DIVISION OF HAY HOUSE

Balboa Press books may be ordered through booksellers or by contacting:

Balboa Press
A Division of Hay House
1663 Liberty Drive
Bloomington, IN 47403
www.balboapress.com
1 (877) 407-4847

Because of the dynamic nature of the Internet, any web addresses or links contained in this book may have changed since publication and may no longer be valid. The views expressed in this work are solely those of the author and do not necessarily reflect the views of the publisher, and the publisher hereby disclaims any responsibility for them.

The author of this book does not dispense medical advice or prescribe the use of any technique as a form of treatment for physical, emotional, or medical problems without the advice of a physician, either directly or indirectly. The intent of the author is only to offer information of a general nature to help you in your quest for emotional and spiritual well-being. In the event you use any of the information in this book for yourself, which is your constitutional right, the author and the publisher assume no responsibility for your actions.

Any people depicted in stock imagery provided by Thinkstock are models, and such images are being used for illustrative purposes only.
Certain stock imagery © Thinkstock.

Printed in the United States of America.

ISBN: 978-1-4525-1258-7 (sc)
ISBN: 978-1-4525-1259-4 (e)

Balboa Press rev. date: 02/19/2014

CONTENTS

PREFACE

This book is for that man, woman, or child who is screaming out, "I've done my best, and my best is just not good enough!"

What a mystery life can be. In searching for success, we can search and strive and still not find the secret. If you're anything like me, you've been searching diligently. The truth is that if you're looking in the wrong direction, it doesn't matter how hard you search; you can look as hard and long as you like, even until the end of the world, and still not find the answer.

To find the answer, you've got to look in the right direction. Once you're looking in the right direction, it's not hard to find the secret, the mystery hidden from the ages.

"Behold it is given unto you to know the mysteries of the kingdom, but to them it is not given. For whoever hath, to him shall be given, and he shall have more abundance: But whosoever has not, from him shall be taken away even that which he hath" (Matt. 13:11–12 KJV).

"Again the kingdom of heaven is like unto treasure hid in a field; the which when a man hath found, he hideth, and for the joy thereof goeth and selleth all that he hath, and buyeth that field" (Matt 13:44 KJV).

If you are looking for the secret to success outside of yourself, you are looking in the wrong direction. The harder you search, the further you are getting from the answer.

The answer you need is you!

You are the answer; you are the secret!

INTRODUCTION

In this book I have adopted a stance that you may not have seen before: a combination of scripturally based faith and positive-thinking philosophy, similar to the Law of Attraction. I've seen many books that profess one or the other, but not both together.

I believe these two belief systems are not mutually exclusive, as some would believe. My interpretation of Scripture tells me they are compatible and actually enhance each other. The fusion of themes has benefited me in my personal life as well as business. I invite you to open your mind to this possibility.

Together with the Bible, self-help books with a spiritual element have been my greatest source of knowledge and inspiration. In fact, they have been my saviour; that is, they have helped me save myself. They have been my coach and mentor, my secret to success. They have enabled me to turn a life of mediocrity and frustration into a life of personal excitement and achievement. They have given me the ability to truly serve others by coaching, teaching, and passing on knowledge that has brought about amazing results in these people's lives.

Knowing that these books are the secret to my success, I have made it a way of life that twice a day, morning and night, I spend time with them. Not just reading them but meditating on them, thinking deeply on them, listening to them. Basically absorbing them mentally and spiritually, making their ideas my ideas, renewing my mind.

One thing I have found consistently is that they are often not straight to the point. Too often there are sections that I find unnecessary. I find myself skipping chunks and then highlighting other parts that get to the nitty-gritty of the matter. Because of this, I thought to myself, *Wouldn't it be great if you had a book that just got straight to the point, a book that had just the stuff that you highlighted?* I think we often make the mistake of overcomplicating things, of majoring in the minors. We clutter our minds with unnecessary information. I know quite a lot of people who have read plenty of self- help books, and while they can hold a good conversation with others about the books, they're not retaining the information that matters, and they're not getting the results they need to bring about change in their lives. In short, they read these books like a novel, because they are written similarly. I don't believe either the Bible or self-help books are meant to be read this way.

For this reason I make no apologies for my book being short and straight to the point. The ideas and philosophies in this book work. They cover a whole range of life issues, from health, to children, to relationships, to money matters. They've worked for myself and the people I've taught, and they'll work for you too if you absorb them and make them your own. So read and reread this book. Meditate on the ideas and think deeply on them. They will change your thinking, and that will change your life.

TAKING CONTROL

Approximately ten years ago, on a freezing July night, the cold, hard truth hit me like a freight train.

No one was coming to my rescue.

On our bedroom floor, my wife was giving birth to our son; he'd come so quickly that we had just called the hospital to tell them we were on our way. But we never made it out of the house.

The complication was that he was breech, and when he had come out to his shoulders, the contractions stopped and he stopped coming. My wife and I stayed calm, but for all my trying, I just could not get his head out. While this was happening, my sister had called an ambulance, but we were stuck in this position for about fifteen minutes before it arrived and were able to fully deliver him.

What I didn't realize was that the umbilical cord was obstructed, and our baby was suffering through asphyxiation. When he was finally born, our boy was blue, and his heart rate was 40 beats per minute, when it should have been 140 beats per minute.

As the paramedics worked on our son, pumping oxygen into his lungs with a hand pump, I went outside to talk to God. I'd been studying faith at a local church for a while and had achieved some small successes. One of the Scriptures that has always impressed me the most is Mark 11:24 "Whosoever shall say unto this mountain, be though removed

1

and be though cast into the sea, and shall not doubt in his heart, but shall believe that those things which he says shall come to pass. He shall have whatsoever he says."

This Scripture told me I had to take responsibility in the situation and not wait for something to happen. I had to make something happen.

I felt strength flow through me as I reminded God what this Scripture said. I told God that I was not going to ask for anything, but that I was going to take control of the situation.

I had a strong belief that parents are supposed to protect their children, not just naturally, but spiritually as well. I also could not accept the idea that a child would be born just to die ten minutes later.

After my conversation with God, I felt fearless and determined. When I went back into the house, the main paramedic pulled me aside and asked me if he could have a word with me. With a grim look on his face and a professional tone in his voice, he told me, "I don't think the little bloke's gonna make it."

This was a defining moment. I refused to become afraid and accept his opinion! Looking directly into his eyes, I replied, "No, he is going to be fine." I know I must have had a look that said I meant business, because the paramedic backed off immediately with a quick reply: "Yer. Okay."

It's amazing how quickly people will change their mind and come into agreement with you when you are clear and absolute about something.

Upon entering the hospital I repeated with conviction, "No, he's going to make it. He's gonna be just fine," to anyone who spoke to me.

As I stood back and watched doctors and nurses buzzing around my son in a hive of activity, things became surreal. A smiling woman in a white coat approached me. "You know, when they called in, I thought they'd be bringing in a dead baby, but it's a miracle. They've done a great job. He's looking good."

Of course, our baby did survive.

But the next day he was placed in intensive care. At a meeting with the head of intensive care, the doctor explained to us that our baby was "fitting" and that this was most likely because he would have suffered brain damage and organ damage due to the lack of oxygen during birth. At this point, once again I reassured the doctor: "No, don't worry; he's going to be just fine." Because of what we had just been through, I thought to myself, *There's no way I'm going to start backing off now.*

About this time we were interviewed by the hospital psychologist, to see how we were handling the fact that our baby would be severely handicapped. After the meeting my wife sneaked a peek at the psychologist's clipboard and notes. Among other things, my wife noticed this statement: "This couple is not prepared for failure." It was not written as a positive statement, but I found it incredibly empowering.

The ward is divided into ten sections. Section one is for the sickest babies and our son was in this section. Some babies are in section one for months, and some never get well. However, within two days our son was in section three; and in three days, he was in section nine. Within another three days we were taking him home in absolutely perfect condition.

Since that time I have pushed myself to learn as much as possible about this incredible power that saved my son's life. What I have learnt I have applied to many different areas of my life; I have used this power to transform my near-bankrupt, failing business into a thriving, prosperous company that has allowed me an income that has totally changed my lifestyle.

I have seen this power make cancer and arthritis completely disappear from people's bodies. I have seen it transform children with learning difficulties and sleeping problems into peaceful, intelligent, happy kids. I have seen it do many incredible, wonderful things in relationships and every area of life. I believe this power controls the world, and I believe it exists for the benefit of mankind.

I truly believe it's the answer to every obstacle we face.

"And you shall know the truth and the truth shall set you free" (John 8:32 KJV).

IF THERE IS HELL ON EARTH, THERE MUST BE HEAVEN TOO

I can barely put into words the emotion I felt as I walked through the hospital room door. The first thing I saw was my perfectly formed, lifeless little boy. He had been placed on a stainless steel trolley right near the door. I remember this so clearly because it made me furious. It felt so wrong for him to be there like that. Time stood still for a moment as I stared at him. He was perfect, he was real; he just wasn't alive. My emotions raced from rage, to despair, to disbelief. I found it hard to control them as I looked over at my beautiful, sad wife being spoken to by the doctor and midwife who had helped her deliver our stillborn baby boy.

I can't remember all the details of that day very well. But I can remember with great clarity the words that were running through my mind: *This will never happen again.*

I decided I would channel my anger into determination and fearlessness.

Jen and I buried our baby boy and made a pact that we would never go through that experience again. We decided we would have another baby and that we would have a boy. We would leave no stone unturned to make sure this next pregnancy and birth would be a success, and that we would have a perfectly healthy baby boy.

We found a book called *"Supernatural Childbirth"* by Jackie Mize that was extremely helpful, as it gave examples of people who had enjoyed problem-free, pain-free pregnancies and deliveries. Their ideas suited me perfectly.

We wrote out a statement about the pregnancy, the birth, and our baby. The statement described exactly how the pregnancy would go—that it would be a joyful, fun experience for everyone in the family, free from all the superstition surrounding pregnancy. Our statement said that our baby would be protected throughout the pregnancy and birth, that no harm would come to him in any way, shape, or form. Our statement said that the delivery would be quick. Our first baby was overdue and had to be induced, and I watched my wife endure an extremely painful labour for nine hours; there were complications that put the baby in a distressed state. But delivery would not be *too* quick. Our second baby had come so quickly that he was born on our bedroom floor. So we wanted enough time to get to the hospital without rushing, but once we got to the hospital, the labour and delivery would be quick, short, easy, and painless.

Twice a day I would read out our statement with enthusiasm and absolute conviction; Jen did the same. Once I had read the statement, I imagined myself standing outside the hospital speaking on my mobile, telling my father what an incredible experience the birth had been, and how perfect our baby boy was.

Our doctor had given us the due date of November 23. My wife mentioned to me that the last week of a pregnancy was extremely uncomfortable, and asked whether I thought we could go for a due date a week earlier. I was very motivated, so I thought, *we've gone this far; let's go for everything.* So we chose the date of birth to be November 14.

At two o'clock in the morning of the fifteenth, Jen woke me to tell me her waters had broken. She had a shower. We called my mother, who lived close by, to come over to look after our children. We then called the hospital to tell them we'd be there shortly. The hospital told us to hurry, given our last child was born at home. But we knew that this time everything would be peaceful.

We arrived at the hospital about thirty minutes later and were given a room to wait in. Jen and I sat and chatted for about twenty minutes. I had a cup of coffee, and Jen had a cup of tea.

It was amazing; my wife was in full labour and not experiencing any pain or stress at all!

In the middle of a conversation she stopped talking and said, "Wait. I'm having a contraction." She closed her eyes for a minute and said, "It's like pressure." About ten minutes later, she had another strong contraction. I called the nurse; she came in and said, "Don't worry; this could take while." She was misled because we were so calm and Jen was in no pain at all. The nurse said, "I'll just check, anyway." She checked Jen's condition. "Oh my goodness, you're fully dilated. We better get you to the birthing room now."

Because our baby was ready, he was very low, so the three of us walked slowly down the corridor to the birthing room. Halfway down the corridor, Jen said, "Wait, wait." We waited for a minute while she had another contraction. No pain, just pressure. Ten more steps and we were in the birthing room. Once in the room, the nurse said, "At least wait for the doctor to get here." She then told me to get Jen's pants off, which I did, as she got things ready for the doctor to arrive. I helped Jen climb up onto the bed, and instantly our baby shot out like a bullet into my arms.

Five minutes later the doctor walked in and made the comment, "I see you don't even need me." *Never a truer word spoken*, I thought. The midwife, who was also pregnant, walked over and, looking at Jen, myself, and our baby, said, "Now that's how you have a baby. I'm gonna have my baby just like that."

Half an hour later I stood outside the hospital making the exact same call I'd imagined every day for the last nine months.

We had a healthy baby boy, born in a pain-free, stress-free childbirth, born three hours later than the date we had decided on.

STEPS TO OVERCOMING SICKNESS

"Fight the good fight of faith."—*1 Timothy 6:12 KJV*

The first and probably greatest step to overcoming sickness is to realize that sickness is an enemy and not a friend and should be treated with an aggressive attitude.

Too many people merely accept someone else's opinion about their symptoms. They lie down without showing any resistance.

But sickness is a thief.

It's a thief that wants to steal your health, your happiness, your quality of life. So you need to treat it like a thief. If you came across someone trying to steal your car, you wouldn't meekly hand over the keys and watch them drive it away. You'd rush over and stop them, attack them if you had to, because you wouldn't let someone take what is rightfully yours.

The same state of mind will overcome all sickness.

Step 1: <u>Understanding</u>

Understand that sickness is an enemy and needs to be treated with disdain, not respect. The power within the human spirit is far greater than any sickness that can come against you.

"For God has not given us a spirit of fear, but of power, and of love and of a sound mind" (2 Timothy 1:7 KJV).

Step 2: <u>Directing our power</u>

Set aside time at least twice a day where you repetitively affirm that the healing power of God is flowing through your body, destroying every symptom of sickness and disease. Do this with as much enthusiasm as possible, injecting life into your words.

Step 3: <u>Concentrating our power</u>

Vividly imagine healing power surging through your body, attacking and annihilating the symptoms that have come upon you. Also imagine telling people how you destroyed the sickness and them telling you how well you look. As you do this, feel the power and peace that you no longer have to fear sickness, because you now have the answer to all health problems.

Step 4: <u>Action</u>

Act as well as humanly possible. Think, speak, and act as congruently as possible. Get your thoughts, words, and actions in harmony with one another. Apply common sense to the doctor's advice; probably the only time you should ignore a doctor's opinion is when he says, "There is no hope."

STEPS FOR OVERCOMING FINANCIAL LIMITATIONS

Generally people who struggle financially suffer from a victim mentality.

Usually they can tell you, with great detail, the exact causes of their financial battles and why they are impossible to overcome. They live in the belief that they are at the mercy of circumstances that are beyond their control. These circumstances can be the economic climate, their lack of education, bad choices, bad timing, or just plain bad luck.

I believe that the Bible tells us that this is an inaccurate view of life, that the truth is the exact opposite. Life, the world, and its circumstances are actually at our mercy, both collectively and individually. They have no choice but to respond to and obey our thoughts, words, and actions.

"I call heaven and earth to record this day against you, that I have set before you life and death, blessings and cursings: therefore choose life, that both thou and thy seed may live" (Deut. 30:19 KJV).

The world and its ways are our creations. Our lives are our creations.

We suffer financial difficulties because we are ignorant of our ability to create life the way we want it.

"Now unto him that is able to do exceedingly abundantly above all that we ask or think, according to the power that worketh in us" (Eph. 3:20 KJV).

11

Step 1: <u>Understanding</u>

The first step in overcoming financial difficulty is eliminating the victim mentality. You are not a victim! Whilst you may be suffering victim like circumstances, this does not accurately reflect who you are. It does accurately reflect your ignorance of the incredible creating power that lies sleeping within every human being.

The Bible tells us, "As in water face answereth to face, so the heart of man to man" (Prov. 27:19). And in Proverbs 23:7 we read, "For as he thinketh in his heart, so is he."

Before we can succeed, we need a personality transformation.

Saturate your mind with Scripture or self-help books or biographies that speak about the power of faith, about the power within the human spirit to overcome. As you do this, you will learn to not fear challenges, but be excited by the prospect of overcoming them.

Now that we recognize that this power is within us, we must activate it and put it to work in our experience. Creative power is released when we think, speak, and act. Generally, these actions are done in an unconscious manner, and our creative power is squandered.

We need to release our power in a definite, organized way.

Step 2: <u>Directing Our Power</u>

Decide what you want to achieve, how much wealth you want, what you want to own, where you want to go, and when you want these things to have happened. Write it down in a clear, concise statement.

Step 3: <u>Concentrating Our Power</u>

Twice a day, preferably morning and night, read this statement aloud to yourself with expectation and enthusiasm.

After doing this for a while, begin to imagine yourself and your life the way they are written in your statement. The object here is to build up a feeling of confidence, power, and excitement. When this is achieved, you are creating your desire.

The degree of emotion you generate determines how powerfully and effectively you create. See "Steps for Generating Positive Emotion" for more details.

Step 4: <u>Action</u>

Sometimes a particular action is needed; sometimes the best action is no action at all. The appropriate action is always one that stimulates your faith and brings about a positive emotion.

Step 5: <u>Awareness</u>

You are now on a crash course with the destiny you have chosen. Be on the lookout for signs that it is manifesting; they are there. Acknowledge them no matter how small or insignificant they may seem. "Seek and ye shall find" (Matt. 7:7).

Get excited by the inches of progress, and pretty soon they will become miles of success. Ignore the inches, and the miles never come.

STEPS FOR PARENTING

A common misconception in bringing up children is the idea that we should judge and treat a child according to his or her behaviour and personality. I believe this is one of the least effective ways to raise children and is actually the cause of many of children's problems.

"Death and life are in the power of the tongue, and they that love it shall eat the fruit thereof" (Prov. 18:21 KJV).

The greatest influence in a child's life is his or her parents. The words you speak and the attitude you have towards your children are a mighty force. Your words, your attitude, and your belief will set your children on a course towards the destiny you have chosen for them. (Most people do this unconsciously.) Until children can think and decide and *believe* for themselves, you are the determining factor in their lives.

Step 1: <u>Decide</u>

Make a definite decision that your children will become successful, strong, well-rounded, secure people (be more specific if it suits you).

Step 2: <u>Bless</u>

Always speak well of your children, regardless of their behaviour. Your words will either *bless* or *curse* your children

Step 3: <u>Persist</u>

Spend ten minutes each morning and night imagining your children fulfilling their dreams and becoming the people you desire them to be.

Step 4: <u>Action</u>

Firmly discipline your children, but always finish the discipline with encouragement, reminding them that everyone makes mistakes and that this in no way means they are failures!

STEPS FOR GENERATING POSITIVE EMOTIONS

No matter what your desire is, there is one key factor that if understood and used properly would create greater intensity in your meditating time and bring about quicker results. This effortless step is often overlooked. Simply put, it is *generating positive emotions* (or feelings).

Most people think that doing confessions or affirmations, meditating, and visualizing is enough. Doing these things is vitally important; don't get me wrong. However, what plants the desires you are believing firmly into your spirit and with greater expectancy are the positive feelings that are generated by the above actions you are taking.

Often I found that for one goal I was really excited; it seemed almost effortless to generate the positive emotions and cause the desire to become more real to me. But in other areas I had to play around a lot more with the tools I was working with, whether due to the fact that the words I used were causing me to remember past failures or that the image I created was directly grating against an issue I was facing that seemed so real. Whatever the case, I took for granted this step, only now realizing how vital it is to the success of those I've been teaching.

It's helpful to think of our emotions as a gauge that lets us know how effective our faith work will be in manifesting our desires. I believe when our state of mind generates a positive emotion, our spirit, which is connected with God, the creative source of the universe, is confirming that we are operating effectively, in accordance with our desires, and that manifestation is in progress!

Keep in mind that we are all designed to have control over our thoughts, words, and actions, but most of us are still underdeveloped when it comes to controlling our emotions. We can gain control of our emotions by the words and scenarios we think of and the references we surround ourselves with. And we can also generate the emotions or feelings that suit us in the same way.

Step 1: <u>Stop</u>

Realize that the way you are feeling is critical to bringing about results. If you are getting anxious or frustrated, or experiencing any other negative feelings, then stop what you are doing, and start doing something different. Tips:

- Use Scriptures that inspire you and remind you of who you are and the abilities that you possess.
- Read over some parts of an inspiring or motivational book that makes you feel good.
- Listen to music that generates positive feelings.

By using steps similar to the above prior to your meditating session, you can save a lot of time. Instead of trying to get the feeling, you would be starting off with a good feeling and building on it.

Step 2: <u>Change</u>

Change your picture or confessions to get you more excited. As stated earlier, sometimes the words or pictures we use cause us to feel negative.

If this is the case for you, try some of the ideas below.

- Change the scenarios. For example, instead of imagining the boss coming and offering you a promotion (since he's been a jerk from the day you met him anyway, and it goes against your normal experience), imagine telling someone you love about the promotion and their excited response.
- Sometimes the future you would like is too much for your imagination to handle and brings about a negative feeling, so start with a small improvement that generates a better feeling. Then, as you are feeling good, gently add more and more detail, expanding your dream to the point where you feel satisfied.
- Use words that get you pumped; sometimes a particular word or phrase may work for one person but make another feel bad.
- It often helps to speak about what you desire in the present tense. For example, instead of saying, "I will be married next year," imagine and confess, "I am married now, I have all my desires now, and I lack nothing."

Step 3: <u>Relax!</u>

Remember, you are creating your future, so start having fun with it. Don't let pressure build up and rob you of the joy this process creates.

YOU MUST DECIDE

Every day the world is waiting, watching, listening. What will you choose next? "I call heaven and earth to record this day against you, that I have set before you, life and death, blessing and cursing: therefore choose life" (Deut. 30:19 KJV).

A great secret to the success of champions is so simple yet a major stumbling block for most people. Champions decide what they want with great passion, and then with absolute conviction they commit to that decision. They refuse to change their minds.

The magic is not in the decision but in the commitment to the decision.

Everyone makes decisions all the time. But to commit to a decision with a spirit that will not take no for an answer, now, not many do that, and that's what makes the world change.

Most people spend a lot of time gathering facts. They mistakenly think that if they have the right facts, they'll be able to make the right decisions. The secret to making a successful decision is not the facts on which you base your decision. The magical power is in your commitment to the decision.

Therefore, the successful choice for you will always be the one you're committed to.

Making a Decision

1. Decide what you want.
2. Commit to that decision daily, with affirmations, visualization, or whatever works best for you.
3. Take logical, appropriate action towards achieving your goal.
4. Be sensitive to inspirational ideas or help from friends or strangers.
5. Persist; be prepared for some temporary setbacks.
6. Do not take no for an answer.

THE WORLD MOVES FOR THE PERSON WHO HAS MADE UP THEIR MIND

Decide what you want and commit to that decision.

Our greatest barrier to success is overcomplicating the process.

We clog up our brilliant hearts and minds with unnecessary and irrelevant facts and information. All that does is weaken our ability and shut down the spiritual genius inside us.

In the story taken from 2 Kings 20:1–6, King Hezekiah was given a message by the great prophet Isaiah: "Set your house in order for thou shalt die, and not live." This was a death sentence from God Almighty himself.

And what did Hezekiah do? He turned his face to the wall and said, "I do not accept this."

He did not meekly say, "Oh well, I guess my time is up." With incredible passion he said, "I want more life!"

Before Isaiah got out of the palace, God told him to go back and tell Hezekiah, "I've heard your prayer, I've seen your passion, and you'll have fifteen more very successful years."

Confusion and doubt are killers.

The necessary requirements for success are singleness of mind, definiteness of purpose, determination, and persistence.

Can it be that simple? What about the million and one details unique to every situation?

When you ask this question, you've stumbled onto the problem. When most people think of "details" unique to their situation, what they really mean are *obstacles*. While you are thinking about these obstacles, you cannot have singleness of mind; you are not being definite. That will weaken your determination, and you certainly won't persist.

That's a fairly accurate description of what a lot of people do when trying to achieve something. Then after doing this for a period of time, they give up and move on to something else, only repeating the same unsuccessful process.

The necessary requirements for success are

- singleness of mind,
- definiteness of purpose,
- determination, and
- persistence.

GOD-GIVEN AUTHORITY

Authority is the power or right to enforce obedience. For authority to be effective it must be properly understood. God has given you all authority over your life. To exercise authority over your life, you must first exercise authority over your mind.

Most people don't have control over their lives because they have not controlled what is being fed into their most precious asset: their heart.

Your mind is constantly being exposed to all kinds of ideas, beliefs, and experiences. These ideas, beliefs, and experiences are then accepted as truth and enter your heart. They then become *your* ideas, beliefs, and experiences.

Most of us were fed the belief, with plenty of examples, that we have no control over our circumstances, that in fact we are at the mercy of our circumstances.

To change our experience we must simply change our minds. To do this we must feed our minds on media that talk about and demonstrate the God-given power of the human spirit. We must shut off exposure to media that tell us we are victims. We must replace it with media that teach us that we are brilliant, powerful, beautiful, and abundant in all areas, lacking in nothing (i.e., God).

After you have saturated your mind with these new amazing truths, you will understand that to master your experience, you only need to master your mind. This state of mind gives you the ability to exercise your God-given authority with amazing results!

GET WISDOM, GET EVERYTHING

"Why is it that I can't get a break?"

"How can it be that I can try as hard as I do, give everything I can and then some more, and still lose?"

"Why is it that I see others put in less than half the effort I do and achieve ten times more?"

"Why? Why? Why?"

Because you are the creator of your reality.

Every thought and every statement is creative.

Every time you ask those questions and make those statements, you proclaim to the universe that you are weak and helpless, a victim of circumstances that are out of your control.

And the universe, which is at your command, says "Yes, sir, right away, sir."

"Give him the experience where nothing works, no matter how hard he tries."

"Oh, except with health, because with health he never makes those statements, he's always saying and thinking, "I never get sick, don't believe in it."

"But everywhere else, make it hard as hell for him."

Negative dialogue running through your mind creates an emotional state of doubt and confusion, and gives birth to your beliefs.

A belief is nothing more than a statement that is run repetitively through your mind. As a statement is run through your mind, it draws to itself emotion and becomes a spiritual force. These spiritual forces leave your mind and create your world.

So the next time you catch yourself worrying and complaining, realize that you are giving commands to your heart to create the very thing you are stating.

God and the universe have only one answer: Yes.

THE ETERNAL LAW OF LIFE

There is an unseen eternal law governing this universe. "I call Heaven and Earth to record this day against you that I have set before you life and death, blessing and cursing: therefore choose life" (Deut. 30:19 KJV).

This law cannot be violated; it is impersonal.

It is neither for you nor against you. It just is.

It can be depended upon, it doesn't change, and it is constant. It is eternal.

Understanding this law makes you extremely powerful. It puts you in control of your life and your destiny. Not understanding this law renders you powerless. It leaves you with the belief that you are at the mercy of circumstances. You become filled with anxiety, fear, and frustration. These are states of being that the universe accepts as your choice and in return will bring you experiences that are worthy of anxiety, fear, and frustration.

So no matter what negative circumstance you may be experiencing, change and success are never far away. With a change of thought and a change of feeling will come a change of experience.

The starting point for change is to receive this truth: that this law *really does exist*! Accept that you are in control, and if you are failing, you have just made some choices in ignorance. Now you're feeling good and ready to make some new, better choices.

Remember, what you *think* and *feel* is what you choose. And the universe is programmed to bring you experiences that match your choices.

GUARD YOUR HEART

Guard your heart, for out of it flow the forces of life.

Your heart is your greatest resource. It is the creative centre of a person. It does not make judgments or have opinions. It is the powerhouse of the human spirit. It creates.

Not understanding this is the source of frustration and *failure*.

What your heart creates is not a decision that it makes, but rather a decision that the conscious thinking mind makes. Your mind is the guard that stands watch over your heart, ensuring that only what is desired is allowed to enter the sacred creative centre of your being.

Your heart has no knowledge of what is being experienced in your environment. It deals only with the knowledge that is passed on to it by the conscious, thinking mind. What is passed on to it can be carefully chosen thoughts, images, and feelings, based on what you want to experience. Or it can be random uncontrolled data, received from your environment via your senses.

Since the day we were born, most of us (nearly everyone) have opened wide the gates of our most treasured possession, our heart. We have ignorantly allowed negative, destructive thoughts, images, and ideas to repeatedly bombard our creative centre. This process has programmed our hearts to bring us mediocrity at best, and misery, failure, and rejection at worst.

This is life-changing information.

Stop the flow of negative stimuli entering your heart, and change the course of your life. Stop focusing on the negative aspects of your environment.

Fix your attention on what you want to believe. Concentrate on information, through books, CDs, tapes, and videos that tell you how great you are and that you can be, do, and have anything you can conceive.

Think, speak, imagine, and feel the way you want life to be, not the way it is. You will bombard your heart with these stimuli and reprogram it with a new agenda.

The greatest man who ever walked the planet travelled around constantly ignoring things the way they were. But He thought, spoke, and acted as though things were the way He wanted them to be. "Calling things that be not, as though they are." (Rom 4:17 KJV) For this He was often misunderstood by the people around Him. He called water wine. He called the dead living. He called a little a lot, feeding more than five thousand people with five loaves of bread and two fish. He programmed His heart for success, while being surrounded by failure. What a success He was!

Success in any situation can never be any further away than a change of heart.

CONFIDENCE IS YOUR GREATEST ALLY. FEAR IS YOUR ONLY ENEMY.

What a trap it is to forget you are the creator of your reality.

It's a terrible state to be lost in your experience, wondering why you are so far from where you want to be, not knowing why you can't get a break or how much work you have to do before you see some sign of success.

I can't think of anything worse than trying everything you know to do and still coming up short, the anxiety of racking your brain with "Where did I go wrong? Why isn't it working?"

That feeling of helplessness is a killer.

I believe such a mental state is a place called hell. It's not a place that you want to stay. If you stay in that place too long, you'll turn nightmares into reality.

"You shall know the truth and the truth shall make you free" (John 8:32 KJV). *Knowing you are the creator of your experience, and how you do it, makes you free!* That feeling of freedom is absolute bliss, heaven— nothing to fear, nothing to worry about. It's the launching pad for an exceptional life.

Grab this truth and hold on to it. Receive it, accept it, and love it. Feel good about it. In fact, make it your daily routine to meditate on it and feel good about it.

As you keep focusing on this truth, your worries will begin to disappear. Your anxiety will begin to transform into peace. Your peace will transform into confidence. Your confidence will transform into boldness, and your boldness will transform into absolute fearlessness. Your personality will be transformed, and you will feel like a new person. Understand, how you feel is incredibly important.

As you think and speak about your future in this state of confidence and peacefulness, circumstances and troubles that you have been trying to change for ages will fade away.

That success that you desperately wanted, but which seemed beyond your grasp, will flow to you effortlessly. *This is because you are the creator of your experience.*

But to create the life you desire you must know it and feel it!

BELIEVE AND SUCCEED

Without belief, everything is hard, so hard that it's impossible.

With belief, nothing is hard; it's easy—no trying, just doing.

What does it mean to believe?

The difference between a normal thought and a belief is the amount of congruent feeling associated with that thought. A thought with a little congruent feeling would be called a weak belief or a wish. A thought with an intense, powerful feeling associated with it would be called a strong belief or a conviction.

"For as he thinketh in his heart, so is he" (Prov. 23:7 KJV). To think in your heart is to think with *feeling*. This is *believing*.

If you want to make changes in your life, you must change what you believe. This is not an easy thing to do if you don't understand how you formed the beliefs you already have. These were formed by information you received from your environment. However, most or all of this was done without conscious effort or control, leaving you at the mercy of whatever environment you happened to have stumbled into.

But if it is true that our beliefs are formed by exposure to a particular environment, and we understand this, we have power to choose what we want to believe. We can control our environment, we can control what we are exposed to, and therefore we can control what we believe. We can also strengthen or weaken beliefs by choosing to focus our attention on specific subjects.

Condition your mind by reading, hearing, and speaking (to yourself). Reading, listening, and speaking will cause you to start thinking and imagining. Thinking and imagining will cause to you start feeling. As you start thinking, imagining, and feeling congruently, you will start to believe.

As you continue this process, your thoughts and imaginations will grow in quantity and quality, and your feelings will become more intense, creating a sense of certainty. Then you will have created a belief or conviction, created by design.

This belief, which is a spiritual force, will control your world, including yourself and everyone in it.

TOTAL CONTROL

If you have no control over your circumstances, you're not controlling your mind. Don't be fooled; you may think, that's just the way life is, but it's not the way life is for everyone. It's the way life is for you. Life is mirroring what is going on inside you. Life is a manifestation of the workings of that secret place that no one sees, your mind. "For there is nothing hid, which shall not be manifested; neither was anything kept secret, but that it should come abroad." (Mark 4:22 KJV)

If that feels like a slap in the face, then you've forgotten who you are. Consider it a wakeup call. If you don't like what you're experiencing, take control of your mind and what you are exposing it to.

Think of your mind as a small child, totally vulnerable to the teachings and influences of its environment. Like an ignorant, innocent little child, it will not say no to negative, destructive influences. Anything that is convincing and consistent it will accept as gospel.

A heavy price will be paid for not keeping guard over this priceless asset. It will bring to you failure and misery just as readily as it will success and joy.

LEARNING TO FLY

Gravity doesn't try to pull you down, a flower doesn't try to bloom, and a bird doesn't worry about how to fly.

A bird is born with an unconscious knowledge that it can fly. It grows up surrounded by brilliant flyers that soar through the sky with ease.

But what would happen to that bird if it was born into a family where they had forgotten how to fly? Where the birds walked because they thought flying was too dangerous and not practical? What if it was told daily that the ability to fly was not for everyone, but only for a few elite birds—that if it struggled and strained as hard as it could, it might just make it one day, but probably not? What would become of that bird and the generations after it?

What you know you are capable of is not *the* truth; it's just *your* truth, and *your truth* is your ceiling; you'll never rise above it.

But what if you knew more? What if you thought you were capable of more? What if you knew that the only limit to anything in your life was whatever you know at any given moment? What if you were being fed daily the belief that you are the creator of your experience— that anything your mind can conceive, it can achieve? What if you surrounded yourself with people who either directly or through books and CDs demonstrated this to be true in their lives?

Then you would change what's true for you.

Then you would know how to live a life that's amazing and outstanding as easily as a bird knows how to fly.

So if you want to learn how to fly, hang out with eagles.

DON'T FAKE IT, FEEL IT

Success in any situation in life is only a feeling away. "He that loveth not knoweth not God; for God is love" (1 John 4:8 KJV).

Access the feeling of love, and you have accessed the power of God.

Often when faced with negative circumstances, we think the circumstance or situation is harming or destroying our lives. We are mistaken.

It's not circumstances that cause us to fail, but how those circumstances make us feel. The *feeling* of *fear* is what destroys us. When we feel fear, we stop the flow of the life-giving force of love: God. When we feel excitement, peace, enthusiasm, power, confidence, contentment, relaxation, happiness, and the like, we have accessed God and released the *irresistible power of love.*

If we are to achieve great success in life, we must first learn the art of maintaining a good feeling in the midst of a negative or hostile environment. This is a skill that the great achievers of our planet have and that the masses have no idea about. This is one of the main reasons that success is so rare and failure so dominant in the majority of people's lives. "For as he thinketh in his heart, so is he" (Prov. 23:7 KJV).

To believe in your heart means to think with a matching or congruent feeling. Thoughts with matching feeling equal believing.

And what you believe, you will receive.

THE ENEMY WITHIN

Over a period of months, I found myself more and more often wondering what had happened. Where had the self-confidence, the feeling of invincibility, the bravado gone? Why had the success that had once been so easy and predictable all but disappeared? And what did I have to do to get it back?

This constant questioning was becoming habitual. The more I searched and wondered, the more helpless I felt. But it wasn't just that I was feeling bad; things weren't working like they once had. "I mean I'm not imagining this. It's just not working anymore. Everything I've achieved I'm losing. I've got to work this out quick."

But nothing changed. The more I wondered and searched, the worse I felt, and the worse things got.

One day as I sat in my usual spot, going over the week's and month's losses, searching for an answer as to where I had gone wrong, there was music playing in the background. I sat there feeling like Superman chained to a huge piece of kryptonite. I started listening to the words of the song that was playing.

Here comes that feeling again.

It's here every day, it's darkness in my face. There's tension in my day.

All my dreams are slipping through my hands. This life is not what I had planned. (These Days, Powderfinger) paraphrased.

It seemed as though the singer knew exactly what I was thinking and feeling and had sung it back to me, as if to say, "Hey, wake up! This is what you are doing."

I thought, *Could it be that I have done this to myself?* Could it be that the voice within my mind, that had once been my champion, had turned on me and become my enemy? Could this voice in my mind be working against me, weakening me, stripping me of my confidence, faith, and strength?

Over the next week I stopped searching, stopped wondering, and stopped all negative talk in my mind. I started making strong, powerful, positive statements about myself and my circumstances, in my mind and aloud, every day. I even spoke and thought with a more authoritative tone.

Over a period of a week my personality changed, and I began noticing how different I felt. Confidence was coming back. The world was changing. Was everything in my world obeying this voice?

The future seemed unlimited once again, and I was looking forward to the challenges of life instead of being afraid of them.

It felt like an old friend who had gone missing had returned, a friend who was fearless and dependable. My greatest friend had returned. Not long after he returned, success in all areas came back as well.

THE ILLUSION OF REALITY

God brings the dead to life, and He does it by "calling things that be not, as though they are." Since the day we were born, we have been taught that we must face the facts: you can't argue with reality.

If this is good advice, then Jesus was the craziest man who ever walked the planet.

What was wrong with that guy? He just couldn't seem to accept reality. He called water wine. He said Lazarus was only sleeping, when he was dead. He called a raging storm peaceful and still. He told a crippled man to stand and walk. He told lepers to go show themselves to the priests, something only done when you were cleansed or healed. He told ten thousand hungry people to sit down so he could feed them with five loaves of bread and two fish. This guy was either completely insane or a genius.

Let's face some facts. The water became wine. Lazarus arose and came to life. The storm became peaceful and still. The cripple stood, picked up his mat, and walked home. The lepers were healed as they went to show themselves to the priests.

The ten thousand hungry people were filled, leaving twelve baskets of leftovers.

Jesus knew the secret behind so-called reality.

He knew the temporary nature of reality and that the source of all reality comes from within the human spirit and is released through thought, word, and action.

Jesus thought, spoke, and acted according to His vision, according to His dream, according to His desire, not according to reality. He was never deceived by the illusion of reality.

Then He said, "These things and more, shall ye do also." Your reality is only as real or permanent as the attention or focus you give it. Think, speak, feel, and act as though your dreams are either here or on their way, and watch your reality shift and change to match them.

How things are is temporary, subject to change.

What is eternal is you, God, and the power to create any reality you desire.

THE NATURE OF COMPETITION

To understand the true nature of competition, you must first understand the principle of unity and oneness in the universe.

Have you ever watched a sporting event where the two teams or opponents are evenly matched in ability? One is the champion, and the other is the newcomer. For three-quarters of the game or match it's neck-and-neck, nothing separating them. Then the champion gets a slight edge, and within a short period of time the newcomer falls to pieces. The champion ends up thrashing his opponent, causing you to forget how close most of the match was. This outcome has nothing to do with their skill and everything to do with what they believe about themselves.

One believes he is a champion; the other believes he might be. Most people would probably agree with this statement. What most people may not realize is that there is another game, a parallel game, going on in the spiritual world.

In the spiritual world there can only be harmony, so when two opposing thoughts come near each other, they must come to some conclusion that allows them to get along. In other words, they must come to an agreement. So in a competitive situation, one thought must submit to the other to have agreement. A superior thought will force all other thoughts to become inferior until it comes up against a thought that says, "No, I will not submit." In this case there is friction momentarily, until what was the superior thought says, "Well, we have to come to an agreement. There cannot be disharmony, so I will have to submit to you."

A new champion is born!

Disunity cannot exist in the spiritual world.

Having this knowledge gives you the strength to be single-minded about your desire and not take no for an answer.

The truth about competition is that there really is no competition.

Once you are settled and steadfast in your mind, everyone and everything will become settled and steadfast with you. When you're uncertain, your experience or environment is uncertain. In speaking about moving mountains, Jesus said to get your eyes off the mountain and onto yourself. It's not about the mountain; it's about you.

You and the mountain are *one*. You are connected; it just looks like you are separated.

Once you are convinced you can move mountains, the mountain will move. To be convinced means to not be double-minded.

To be single-minded simply is to stop changing your mind. This is faith.

Keep choosing the same thing, and feel good knowing that you are one with the world, so your choice must become the world's choice.

THE IRRESISTIBLE POWER OF LOVE

Nothing on the planet can resist love.

If you are facing obstacles that are stopping you from living the life you desire, you need to *love them to death!*

In the presence of love, obstacles melt away.

Love is the force that will destroy every obstacle standing in your way. This is because "faith worketh by love" (Gal. 5:6).

Most of the time when we try to tackle a problem in our lives, whether it be financial lack, sickness, relationship breakdowns, or any other kind of trouble, in trying to change it we are usually focused on all its negative aspects. As we focus on these negative aspects, instead of feeling confident and powerful, we feel terrible, weak, and afraid. So the force that's emanating from us is usually fear, worry, resentment, or hatred.

These forces are definitely not love, and they are never going to change that situation positively. In fact, they are going to add to it and strengthen it in its negativity. You may think this what you should be doing, because you think you have got to address the situation to change it. But this the last thing you should be doing.

Where there is no love, there is no faith!

So, what is love?

The Oxford English Dictionary tells us that "to love is to have passionate desire and affection for, that love is an intense emotion of affection".

If you have had trouble getting your faith to work for you, or you have had some problem that you just can't seem to move, remember the way you have been feeling when you think about the situation you're trying to change. If you have been trying for a while and that situation has not changed, I guarantee it's because of your negative feelings.

You need to find ways of thinking and speaking about that situation that bring forth positive feelings. The more positive feeling, the more power. The more power, the quicker the change.

Often when we think we are addressing a problem, we are actually just worrying about it. So it will help just to forget it altogether and focus on something that's going well in life.

Just by not adding to the problem with your negative emotion, you will see a change take place. Then, after focusing on what's working in your life and thinking good feeling thoughts for a while, you may feel you can address the problem in a new way that stimulates a positive feeling.

When you can think of that negative situation and feel excitement, power, enthusiasm, or peace, you feel the power of love, and faith works by love.

Love will bring failure to its knees.

SURROUNDED BY LOVE

God's love is not some religious mumbo-jumbo.

It is real, and it surrounds us everywhere we go and at all times.

Love is God's gift to us. It is the power to receive anything we need or desire, and it *is* the thing we need or desire!

He sent you Love, and we receive that Love as the thing we are believing for!

"God is love" (1 John 4:8 KJV). "Faith works by love" (Gal. 5:6 KJV).

No matter where we are or what we are facing, nothing can separate us from the love of God. It is always present in all circumstances, everywhere.

When we are focused on our troubles and what we don't want, we are in fear and shut ourselves off from being able to receive that love. But it is still there with us. The minute we turn from our fears and put our attention on our dreams and desires, we flick the switch, and that love that surrounds us begins to flow into our lives. As we focus our attention on receiving the things and experiences we desire, whether we are speaking, visualizing, daydreaming, or planning, we are accessing the power of God, and we know it because we can feel it.

First Corinthians 13:13 famously reminds us, "Faith, hope, love, and the greatest of these is love."

Hope is deciding what you want.

Faith is the knowledge that you can and will have this thing that you want.

Love is that powerful, positive *feeling* born out of the knowledge that you are receiving your desire.

Stop worrying and shutting yourself off from the answer that you so desperately want. Start thinking and feeling good about receiving all those great things that are already yours; they are with you now and always have been.

You are surrounded by them.

ARE YOUR BELIEFS TRAITORS?

"For the thing which I greatly feared is come upon me, and that which I was afraid of is come unto me. I was not in safety, neither had I rest, neither was I quiet; yet trouble came" (Job 3:24–25 KJV).

Actions without belief will never be effective. Why?

Because belief rules experience.

Job took action. According to his religion, they were the right actions to take. They worked for many others and should have worked for him. But while he was taking the right actions, he was thinking failure (worrying) and feeling afraid (fear). *What he was thinking and feeling controlled what showed up in his experience. His actions could not overcome his belief.*

So many times in life we try to find the right actions to change our experience, to bring us success. Just as Job did, we try to change our actions until we find one that works. We try doing the same thing different ways. Or we try doing completely different things. Some of us find a way that works, and some of us die trying.

But there is another way: *Realize that your beliefs are causing your actions to fail,* (which is why the same actions work for others).

So instead of altering your actions in search of success, change the limiting beliefs that are sabotaging them.

Once you have decided what you want to achieve, you must have beliefs that support your endeavours. Your beliefs will cause your actions to be incredibly effective; they will cause fortunate circumstances to come your way. They will cause new ideas to pop into your mind. What was complicated will become simple. Your beliefs will literally carry you to your dream.

So what is a belief?

A belief is just a thought that is run repetitively through your mind with some degree of congruent emotion. It can be based on experience, yours or someone else's. It can be based on something you have heard, seen, or read. It can be based on anything, actually, which is why we often think someone else's beliefs are crazy. Often beliefs are nothing more than mental habits.

If you're having trouble getting things to work out, and your efforts are not effective, look into your mind.

Throw out those old, weak, insipid beliefs that are hiding in your mind. They are traitors, and they have to go. Replace them with life-giving beliefs that will empower you to achieve your dreams.

Try some of these:

"All things are possible to him that can believe" (Mark 9:23 KJV).

"I have favour with God and man" (Luke 2:52 KJV).

"With long life will He satisfy me" (Ps. 91:16 KJV).

"The Lord renews my youth like the eagles" (Ps. 103:5 KJV).

"By Jesus stripes I was healed" (2 Pet. 2:24 KJV).

"I am guarded in all my ways by angels, and they lift me up so I won't even dash my foot against a stone" (Ps. 91:10–12 KJV).

"I can do all things through Christ which strengthens me" (Phil. 4:13 KJV).

"I let the peace of God rule in my heart and I refuse to worry about anything" (Col. 3:15 KJV).

"And I having received the gift of righteousness do reign as a king in life" (Rom. 5:17 KJV).

"Nothing can separate me from the love of God" (Rom. 8:39 KJV).

PASSION AND RESPONSIBILITY

You will never meet a successful person who is a victim and lacks passion. You will never meet a failure who takes responsibility and is passionate about what he or she does.

This is not a coincidence!

All extremely successful people always have two outstanding qualities in their character.

1. Responsibility: that is, they are not a victim. They believe they have control over their circumstances, and if things aren't right, they will look to see where they themselves are in error.
2. Passion; they have intense enthusiasm and love for what they do. They may not know they have these qualities, they may not understand these principles, or they may be doing them unconsciously. But they will always have these two qualities, and if they ever lose either of them, their success will disappear.

When you accept responsibility for why things are the way they are, you will experience two incredible emotions. The first one is relief or peace, because you realize there's nothing to be afraid of. If this is all you do, with the absence of fear alone, your quality of life will begin to improve immediately. Many of your negative experiences will cease to happen.

After the emotion of peace will come excitement or passion; that is to say, *love*. "Faith worketh by love" (Gal. 5:6 KJV).

This love or passion that you now feel for your desires is the power of God, and as you focus and refocus on your desires with this power operating through you, the universe will respond, bringing to you all the necessary ingredients for your desire to manifest.

Remember, love = passion = God = power.

These four words are interchangeable.

YOU ARE BRILLIANT.
YOU ARE A BORN CREATOR.

You have had awesome creative power since the day you were born: the power to have or be anything you can imagine. Not understanding this is the greatest downfall of mankind.

We kill, steal, and destroy to get the things we think we desperately need, because we feel we must. We think there is no other way to get what we desire. And all our lives, the things we think we need are inside of us, waiting and ready to be brought into manifestation.

We read in 2 Peter 1:2–3, "Grace and peace be multiplied unto you through the knowledge of God and of Jesus our lord. According as his divine power has [that's past tense] given unto us all things that pertain unto life and godliness, through the knowledge of him that calls us to glory and virtue."

You don't have the things, but you do have the *power* to get the things! The power is in the *knowledge.* Knowledge is knowing that all things already exist in their raw form, *energy* or *thought.*

Take responsibility for whatever messes you've created, and you'll be set free—free to consciously create the incredible life you desire and deserve. Trust yourself; trust the power within you. It hasn't let you down yet! Only you can let it down, with ignorance.

Hosea 4:6 says, "My people are destroyed for a lack of knowledge."

It's no harder to create the life we dream of having than it is to create whatever mess we have now.

All we need is the revelation that we are the ones creating it all.

THE TRANSFER OF THOUGHTS

Being influenced by certain people and certain environments has caused us to think what we think and believe what we believe. These influences have shaped our personality and are the cause of the state of mind we walk around with on a daily basis. Of course, the great secret is that our state of mind, or personality, determines what we experience.

Who we are—or, more accurately, who we think we are—determines what we can achieve and have.

I doubt that many of us, if any, chose our influences very wisely or even consciously. They were more likely thrust upon us at an early age, before we could do anything else but accept them and then learn to embrace them.

Then, at a later stage in life, we looked at ourselves and our predicament and wondered, *how the hell did I get here!*

But it's never too late to change your influences, role models, and teachers.

Choose your teachers carefully, based on what they've done and what they have achieved. Are they the type of person you would like to be, are they getting the sort of results you would like to achieve, and do they have the type of life you would like to have? Once you have worked this out, hang out with them; associate with them as much as possible. Allow them to *influence* you, and be *persuaded* to believe what they believe.

Through close association you will replace your unwanted ideas, thoughts, and beliefs. They will be replaced with the mindsets and attitudes of winners. You will become a new person as you absorb theses forces.

The magic is that you don't just get a new set of thoughts; you get a whole new experience.

Basically, you'll get the results they get.

RULE OR BE RULED

"He that has no rule over his own spirit is like a city that is broken down, and without walls" (Prov. 25:28 KJV).

Without conscious thought, definite decisions, and plans, your mind will be infiltrated by its environment. If you haven't taken a stand and made an absolute decision in a particular area of life, you've decided to go with the flow. Your culture, your family, and your friends have ideas and beliefs about life. Where you don't rule your mind, these ideas and beliefs will become your ideas and beliefs, and your heart will produce an experience that matches them.

A city is a production centre, and cities used to be protected by high walls against attacking enemies. As long as the walls were strong and guarded, enemies could not enter the city. But if the walls were weak and unguarded, enemies could easily enter and take control.

Your plans, your decisions, and your beliefs are what guard your spirit or city, your production centre.

It may seem like you are having an experience very much like those around you, as in when a depression hits the economy and you're laid off work along with lots of others, or you catch a virus that's going around. Because your experience is so similar, you can easily think, *I didn't do this.* But the truth is your experience is totally unique to you. It just looks similar because the same thoughts that entered those around you entered your unguarded city.

Your future is as sure as the decisions you have made about it and the commitment you have made to those decisions. *What happens to you is up to you.*

Who is ruling the most valuable resource you own, your mind?

Is it you, or is it your culture in disguise?

1. Recognize that you are the only one who creates in your life.
2. Guard your mind from invading thoughts and beliefs of those around you.
3. Make your own decisions about your life and future, and put them in a written statement.
4. Twice a day affirm and visualize, with feeling, the fulfilment of your plans.
5. Do not take no for an answer.

WHY IS IT TAKING SO LONG?

"For nothing is secret, that shall not be made manifest; neither anything hid, that shall not be known and come abroad" (Luke 8:17 KJV).

If you want to know what's going on in that hidden, secret place called your mind, take note of what's showing up in your experience. I believe that often life seems to be so mysterious because we are unaware of what's going on in our secret place (mind).

Many times after struggling in certain areas of life, it has finally dawned on me that for years I'd thought that these areas were tough, or unattainable, or just harder than other parts of life. I'd been doing this for so long that it had become habitual, and therefore I was doing it unconsciously. I'm sure many people have had a similar experience.

These negative beliefs started out as a single thought. They became strong beliefs after they were rerun and rehearsed many times in my mind.

A belief is nothing more than thinking the same thing over and over. Think it once, it's a thought. Think it a thousand times, it's a belief.

Therefore, to have a strong belief is to be single-minded. *This is what all champions do; they just keep thinking the same thing.* No matter what they have just experienced, such as failure, they don't change their minds.

If thoughts are creative, then the secret to success is to stop changing your mind.

Winners keep choosing the same thing (success), and whenever you're winning, you do too.

GET A LIFE

Feeling dull, bored, or depressed will cause heart failure.

If you're not feeling excited, either you've taken your eyes off your dream or you haven't got one.

You must have a dream or vision for your life that is exciting and makes you feel passionate. Dreams and goals are life-giving—not so much the achieving of them as the journey to them. The style of living they invoke is the only way to satisfy your spirit.

Most people try to satisfy the spirit with the pathetic goal of getting their bills paid. This will cause your heart to shrivel from starvation and put you in an early grave. "Hope deferred maketh the heart sick, but when desire cometh it is a tree of life" (Prov. 13:12 KJV).

You're not fully alive until you feel the thrill of setting yourself challenges and overcoming them. This process causes you to grow and evolve as a being. It forces you to become more than you were. *This is living*, not just maintaining, not just existing.

The setting of a goal and attempting to achieve it does wonders for your self-esteem, for in your striving to achieve, you are sending messages to your subconscious that you are a motivated person of substance, definitely going somewhere.

The person without a goal or dream knows either consciously or unconsciously that he or she is going nowhere. Of course, this brings about a state of unhappiness, anxiety, or helplessness. These states of being will bring a life of failure and heartbreak.

It's about the journey, not the destination.

Get a dream! Get a life of excitement!

NEW YEAR MESSAGE

(This message was originally written at the end of the year, but of course it's important to realize that every day is a new day and a new opportunity to start a plan for the future. Please don't wait for particular days on the calendar to create your future. Now is the perfect time.)

With the New Year fast approaching, now is the time to decide what the year ahead will bring. By the end of this year, what will we have accomplished? Will we look back and say, "This was the year I broke through. This was the year I got it figured out? That this was the year I realized there's nothing standing between me and my dreams, just the ability to match positive feeling with my visualization, words, and ideas? That this was the year I learnt 'the art of believing'?

I believe there's absolutely nothing standing between you and your desires. I don't care what you are experiencing or what obstacles seem to be in your way; you have everything that is required to get you from where you now stand to the fulfilment of your dream.

Of course you can never reach your destiny if you don't know what it is you want to accomplish. So decide where you're going to be at the end of this year. Write a short statement saying what you will accomplish. Make a commitment to spending at least twenty minutes twice a day experiencing internally the manifestation of your vision.

Experiment in your imagination with different scenarios; expand on your dream or perhaps phase it back a notch or two.

Look at it from different angles. Look at it when it's half-finished or when it's completely fulfilled. See it from a spectator's point of view, watching the scene unfold before you, or be there inside yourself fully experiencing the moment.

Maybe don't see it at all, but affirm it with references repeatedly.

Which one of these actions works best? They all work. But the one that will work the best for you is the one that makes you feel positive, whether with enthusiasm, excitement, power, or peace.

As you feel that emotion, return again and again to that vision or statement. When you focus and refocus on your dream, stimulating positive feeling, you are accessing the creative power of the universe, the power of God.

The first sign of manifestation is that more and more thoughts and ideas will come to you. Soon after that you will see signs that your belief is affecting the world, and your level of excitement will increase, because as well as achieving your goal, you are growing in the awareness that *you* really are in control of *your destiny*. This is perhaps the greatest achievement of all.

U M I

Lack of connectedness, that feeling of separation, is the downfall of many otherwise-competent and intelligent individuals.

<u>*Separation is an illusion.*</u>

"One God and father of all, who is above all, and through all, and in you all" (Eph. 4:6 KJV). God is the energy through which we are all intimately connected.

I believe it was this connection that Jesus had in mind when He instructed us to love our neighbours as ourselves and when He made the statement, "And whoso shall receive one such little child in my name receiveth me." (Math 18:5 KJV)

All through the Scriptures and other important writings, we see the philosophy that when we behave a certain way, the world will mirror that behaviour, as in "give and it shall be given." (Luke 6:38 KJV)

When you meditate on this idea, and see the truth in it, you will unlock the door to tremendous personal power. You will see that the world is not standing in your way, but waiting for your command!

You are connected to that irritating neighbour.

You are connected to your boss.

You are connected to your car.

You are connected to the traffic you drive in.

You are connected to your clients.

You are connected to the weather.

You are connected to your household appliances.

You are connected to strangers.

You are connected to your enemies.

You are connected to your friends.

A shift in your consciousness will cause a shift in your circumstances, your world. It has to, because you are one with your world.

There is no place where you end and the world begins.

That mountain that appears to be standing in your way is one with you. Grasp this truth, and you'll see the mountain step aside.

YOUR POWER IS NOW

"Now faith is the substance of things hoped for, the evidence of things not seen" (Heb. 11:1 KJV).

Whether you're thinking about yesterday, pondering the events of today, visualizing your future in ten years' time, or remembering an experience in your childhood, you are creating *now*, in this current moment.

The creative powerhouse within you, your heart or spirit, is always active in the present tense. It is always in the present time zone of *now*.

I believe the reason that so many people's lives seem to never change much after the age of eighteen is that their thoughts are generally on today and yesterday. Most of their time for thought is spent pondering the events of the current week and the weeks gone by, so there is a familiar theme to their lives.

The names and faces may change, but similar people and events keep coming into their lives, as if they are walking through a revolving door. Things are constantly changing; they just keep changing to the same thing.

Your *heart* or *spirit* doesn't discern between what you do want and what you don't want. It doesn't discern between past, present, or future. It doesn't discern between true and false (whatever that is), realistic and unrealistic. That is the job of your conscious thinking mind. Your heart responds to thoughts and feelings.

Now read this passage very carefully: Whosoever shall say unto this mountain, be thou removed and be thou cast into the sea; and shall not doubt in his heart but shall believe that those things which he says shall come to pass; he shall have whatsoever he says. Therefore what things soever you desire, when you pray, believe that you receive them and you shall have them. And when you're praying forgive if you have anything against anybody; that your father which is in heaven may forgive you. But if you do not forgive, neither will your father in heaven forgive you. (Mark 11:23–26KJV)

Praying is thinking with emotion.

Remembering is thinking with emotion.

Believing is thinking with emotion.

This is how the human spirit creates. Whatever you are experiencing or have experienced is of no relevance to your heart. It is *not* responding to your experiences. It is a creation machine, and it *is* responding to your thoughts and feelings.

Your thoughts and feelings are taken as your desire, your command, and acted upon.

Don't fool your heart by remembering past failures and hurtful experiences. Create an incredible future by rehearsing your past successes in great detail, generating a feeling of excitement and confidence! Tell your heart that you are an outstanding achiever!

These thoughts and feelings of success and happiness are accepted as *belief* and taken as your command for the future.

What you are thinking and feeling now is all that matters.

AFFIRMATIONS: THOUGHTS TO SAY AND MEDITATE ON

Success

"God has made all grace abound toward me, success in all things is flowing to me constantly" (2 Cor. 9:8 KJV).

"Nothing can separate me from the love (power) of God and He has freely given me all things" (Rom. 8:32, 35 KJV).

"I delight myself in the Lord and He gives me the desires of my heart" (Ps. 37:4 KJV).

"And I having received the gift of righteousness do reign as a king in life" (Rom. 5:17KJV).

"In all things I am more than a conqueror, through Him that loved me" (Rom. 8:37 KJV).

Health

"The same spirit that raised Jesus from the dead lives in me and destroys every symptom of sickness and disease. My body is in perfect health" (Rom. 8:11 KJV).

"No sickness shall come near my household" (Ps. 91:10 KJV).

"I declare over all my family that we were healed by the stripes of Jesus, and everyone's body is in perfect health" (1 Pet. 2:24, Ps. 107:20 KJV).

"The Lord forgives all my iniquities and heals all my diseases" (Ps. 103:3 KJV).

"The Lord will satisfy me with long life" (Ps. 91:16 KJV).

"The Lord renews my youth like the eagles and my body is in a youthful state" (Ps. 103:5 KJV).

Protection

"No evil will befall me; neither shall any disaster come near my family… For we are guarded in all our ways by angels and they lift us up so we won't even dash our foot against a stone… A thousand may fall at our left side, ten thousand at our right hand, but no harm will come near us" (Ps. 91:7,10–12).

Children

"My children are the head and not the tail, they shall be above only and not beneath… They are blessed coming in and blessed going out" (Deut. 28:6,13).

"Great is the peace of my children, for they are taught of the Lord" (Isa. 54:13).

Peace

"When I lie down I shall not be afraid, I shall lie down and my sleep shall be sweet" (Prov. 3:24).

"The peace of God, which passes all understanding, keeps my heart and mind, and I refuse to worry about anything" (Phil. 4:7).

"I let the peace of God rule my mind" (Col. 3:15).

Repeat these thoughts to yourself, speaking with passion and conviction, generating feelings of confidence, power, and excitement. Or just quietly mull them over, allowing them to sink deeply into your mind. Do whichever feels best, which will change, depending on what's happening in your life.

They will become beliefs, changing your personality and transforming your circumstances.

TESTIMONIES

Overcoming Cancer

In 2003, at the age of fifty-six, I was diagnosed with breast cancer. At first I refused to have any treatment. I wasn't afraid of cancer or afraid to die, but I was terrified of any treatment I would have to undergo. My two daughters and other family members pleaded with me to at least try. So I said I would go one round, all the time believing I would die.

Then a cousin of mine took me along to meet Shayne, who then started to teach me how to have true faith. Shayne gave me several affirmations to say to heal the body, but also told me without true faith and positive thinking and feelings I would be wasting my time. So I decided I had nothing to lose and a life to gain.

I spent many hours meditating, seeing myself well and hearing my breast surgeon telling me the cancer was gone. After three months of chemotherapy, the surgeon wanted to take my breast off, but I refused, telling her that I no longer had cancer. She then asked me why I would think such a thing was possible. So I told her about Shayne and what I had been doing.

She said, "That's well and good, but I have removed ten lymph nodes, of which seven were cancerous, and *cancer that extreme* doesn't go away after three months of chemotherapy."

We reached an agreement. She would put me into hospital and remove more breast tissue for testing. If there was any sign of cancer, I would have my breast off.

Five days after the test, I returned to the surgeon for my results.

She handed me my pathology report and told me to "take it home and frame it."

There was *no sign of any cancer*, and she had never seen anything like that before.

I am very grateful to my daughters, family, and friends for all their love and support, but without Shayne and his wife, Jen, taking me into their home and teaching me how to have real faith and always think positively, I have no doubt this testimony would have a very different ending.

I have now been in remission for five years.

Maureen Anderson
Melbourne, VIC

Young Man Finds Hope

Over the years I have studied faith with Shayne, and I have received many great victories. I first came to Shayne's when I was nineteen years old. At the time I couldn't hold a relationship; I was constantly angry and was very annoyed with the hand that was dealt to me in life. I was a thin, angry young man who was spinning out of control.

My girlfriend was no longer interested in me, and I couldn't give up smoking despite many attempts, which lasted no longer than a day or two.

While driving, I constantly exceeded the speed limit and regularly suffered road rage.

Upon first applying the principles of faith, at a predetermined time of the day, I would fill my mind with wealth, love, and self-control. Within a few days, my life began to transform. I became inspired to catch thoughts of anger and frustration, because I knew that they were the cause of the circumstance. I replaced them with thoughts of wealth and love. Thoughts of failure I replaced with success, and amazing results followed.

I completely cut sickness out of my life; although symptoms would come, I would reject them and believe in health and strength.

I became exceedingly confident and stabilized the relationship that was on the brink of failure. We've now been together over six years, recently engaged, and still going strong.

I advanced quickly in my studies and have kicked off a career with large frequent pay rises.

I have massive hopes and desires for my future, which allow me to waken with passion and enthusiasm for my day. I have incorporated faith (affirmations and visualizing and believing) into my daily habits, which allows me to see results daily. Overall it continues to inspire me as it leads me into a new chapter of my life, which is more alive and driven than I previously could have hoped for.

Jake Dorian
Brisbane, QLD

Overcoming as a Parent

I began attending Shayne's faith meetings after going through almost two traumatic years with my five-year-old daughter. She had a severe behavioural problem, so bad that the school she was attending in prep asked her to leave. For over one year she had been physically hurting other children, teachers, adults, and herself. She would bite, punch, and kick others. She would hit her head on the floor and pinch herself. She would rarely show remorse, and lash out at anyone who tried to pull her into line. At such a young age all her carers where concerned that she had some form of learning or behavioural problem; ADHD was a favourite among her teachers, after meeting with different people at the school and hearing their grim diagnosis: that whatever it was would be with her for the rest of her life. My desperation grew, and I was ready to try anything to help my little girl have a better life. You see, through growing up as a Christian, I have a strong belief that God doesn't give children disabilities or psychological problems. I knew God had provided for her healing. I just had no idea how to make it manifest. After attending one of Shayne's meetings, I decided I had nothing to lose and everything to gain. Straight away I started putting into practice what I had learnt.

Shayne and his wife talked me through what I needed to do, gave me specific Scripture and steps to help reinforce this new belief: that my daughter was an easy-going, well-behaved girl with lots of friends and that her teachers loved her.

Results began to appear almost immediately; within a year her behaviour had completely changed. Now nine years old, she is a sweet, polite, confident, well-adjusted girl, who is doing well in school and has lots of friends. I often watch her play or read a book and marvel at the miraculous working power that lies within us all.

I thank God for Shayne and Jen.

Elisha McKenzie
Melbourne, VIC

ABOUT THE AUTHOR

My school years were very frustrating. I remember as a student often having the thought, *"I'm just not up to it. I just don't get this stuff.*

What a terrible feeling it is when you know you have given your best and your best is simply not good enough. It's one thing to have not put in the effort you should have and to come up short. You feel disappointed, maybe even guilty. It's an entirely different thing when you have given something the best you have and yet you're not even close to succeeding. It can be crushing to know you just haven't got what it takes.

My family moved a lot during my childhood, so I went to many, many different schools, and some of those schools two or three times. My education suffered with all the moving, so I was only an average student. As a result, many times I thought, *I'm just not good enough for things like maths and science*, and my results were poor. Moving school so many times did instil in me toughness; I had an us-against-them fighting attitude. School children can be very mean and cruel to the new kid. It seemed every time I started a new school, I would get tested. You either get used to being picked on—not a pleasant idea—or you learn how to handle yourself.

In my teen years it seemed like I was fighting in the street just about every weekend. Since I was doing so much fighting, the obvious answer was that I get good at it. My father had enjoyed a short professional boxing career, so I asked him to train me to fight. As an amateur I had a reasonable boxing career, winning a state title. The trouble began when

I turned pro. After a successful start in my professional career, full of promise and potential, I began to lose fight after fight. Once again I felt that crushing feeling of "I'm just not good enough." I thought more effort was the answer. In fact, I thought more effort was the answer to just about everything. The problem was that the more I strove and strained, mentally and physically, the worse my results. After years of unsuccessful attempts and lots of blood, sweat, and tears, I wore myself out. I put it down to a mystery I didn't know the answer to.

I had a similar trend in my business life. I tried one business after another. They all seemed to start off with great potential, but then hard times would hit, and the struggle would begin.

Every step of the way life seemed tough. That was the theme of my life for the first thirty years.

My search for why life was so hard and success so elusive led me to reading and studying. I began to put my best efforts into searching the Scriptures and other books. After years of study and practicing what I have learnt, I have achieved some of the most incredible and quite amazing successes, many of which people would struggle to believe could happen.

I believe I now know the answers to the mystery of my successes and failures.

I think they will be the answers to the mysteries of your successes and failures.